The Miracle of Change

A Book for Young Ladies

"Daughter of the King"

Written by: Ami M. Loper
Illustrated by: Carol J. Loper

Copyright   © Ami Loper

Miracle of Change - A Book for Young Ladies
Published 2007
by Biblical Standard Publications
Maggie Valley, NC

in Coordination with
Dream Builders, LLC
1026 W. Woodman Dr.
Tempe, Az 85283
miracle-books@cox.net
http://members.cox.net/miracle-books/

All rights reserved. No portion of this publication may be reproduced, or transmitted in any form by any means - electronic, mechanical, photocopying, or any other - except for brief quotations, without the prior written permission of the author.

Electronic Layout Design: Tim Loper

ISBN 978-0-9678798-2-6

Acknowledgments...

With all my heart I wish to thank my precious husband, Tim, without whose persistence, vision, encouragement, and sacrifice this book would never have come to be. Thank you for believing in me, my Love. Thank you to my truly beautiful daughters who helped me in the refining process. A special thank you to Carol & Dave who made this sacrificial gift just "because we're family." My undying gratitude to Gary & Anne Marie Ezzo for showing us a better way. And many thanks to my many editors and encouragers: Anne Marie Ezzo, Cris Crawford, Kate Fuller, Dr. Ron Jones, Carla Link, and, of course, Inice Hahnke, Tammy King, Brenda Markey, and Pat Singleton.

My highest thanks and praise to Jesus Christ, who allowed me to hold the pencil as He wrote the book. To Him be all the Glory. Psalm 115:1

~Ami Loper

Dear Parent,

Congratulations! Your daughter is growing into a young lady. I know you are doing all you can to prepare her for the journey. I applaud your courage and devotion. It takes courage to have the important discussion concerning the changes your daughter will soon face, and it takes devotion to her and to God to not allow anyone to take your place, but to teach her yourself. Walking through this time in your daughter's life will bring you two together on a new level and you will both be blessed by the process.

As with my prior book, The Miracle of Life, this book is intended to be a companion to Reflections of Moral Innocence by Gary and Anne Marie Ezzo. The Miracle of Change focuses in on a specific piece of the puzzle that will comprise your teaching of the 'facts of life.' Reflections of Moral Innocence will give you a complete look at all the pieces of this education process. To find more information on how you can obtain a copy of this material, please visit www.gfi.org.

In the book, The Miracle of Change, A Book for Young Ladies, we will discuss the changes your daughter will be experiencing in puberty. As the mother of three daughters, I can attest to the fact that the how and when of reading this book are very individual questions that can only be answered by an attentive parent. Each girl is different and will require her parent to approach this subject in a manner reflecting her uniqueness. This advice is true particularly when choosing how fast or slow the information is given, how casually or gently the information is given, and exactly when the information is given. Each of my own daughters received this information at different ages and with different approaches.

Puberty will be a delicate time in your daughter's life that must be handled with great care. Take into account the personality of your daughter in the way you approach these issues. While some girls may take all the information in stride, others may be much more sensitive. Make sure the utmost discretion is used. Do nothing that may embarrass this future woman.

Choosing the timing for the reading of this book with your daughter will require a watchful eye. Although most girls begin their periods around twelve or thirteen years of age, some girls start much earlier and can become very alarmed if not appropriately informed.

Watch your daughter's development. Though there is no way to know exactly when a girl will begin to menstruate, there is generally a predictable sequence to development. The first menstrual cycle should begin a year or so after the breasts begin to develop. This is not always the case, but it is recommended that if your daughter begins to show signs of early development, instruction should follow closely behind.

Your daughter may have many questions that are not answered in this book. Talking with your child about the birds and the bees is not a one-time discussion. It ought to be progressive, in that the child should not be overwhelmed by receiving all the information at one time. Talking about the flower when your child is young should flow into a frank but gentle discussion about her changing body years later. It may again be years before she is even curious about the more detailed facts of sexuality.

Be open to answering the questions your daughter has during this talk without burdening her with information she does not need to know at any given point. Again, I would refer you to the <u>Reflections of Moral Innocence</u> series for a more comprehensive guide for teaching about these issues and for help in determining the appropriate timing to convey new information. The wise parent dispenses information as it is needed; she does not flood her child with a barrage of premature facts.

In <u>The Miracle of Change</u>, I have made every effort to present the changes that will occur during puberty in a positive light. Please grant your daughter the freedom to enjoy all the aspects of her approaching womanhood without the taint of a "curse" mentality when it comes to menstruation. Eve may have been cursed at the Fall of Man, but if we have accepted Jesus as our Lord, we are redeemed women whose Savior died for all curses. Your daughter deserves to grow in the light of joy and hope that comes from knowing that womanhood and all it entails is a blessing.

Before reading <u>The Miracle of Change</u> with your daughter, please read through it yourself. Reacquainting yourself with the facts may be helpful. You will also want to know all that is covered in the book. If there is information you feel your daughter is not ready for, simply omit it for the time being. Second, if possible, I recommend that you read (or re-read) <u>The Miracle of Life</u> with your daughter as <u>The Miracle of Change</u> is really a continuation of that book.

Because communication is the lifeline of a healthy parent-child relationship in the middle and teen years, please make every effort to encourage openness. Take breaks throughout the reading to discuss any questions. If your daughter seems quiet, you may want to try some probing, open-ended questions such as, "What have you heard about this already?' or "How does this make you feel?" Don't be in a rush as you read this book. Set aside a good segment of time for just the two of you to be alone without interruptions. Make the situation as relaxed as possible.

Be sure, as you wrap up your time together, to leave the door open to any further questions or discussions. Prayer is an excellent way to close the discussion. Our children need to know that God is involved in every aspect of our lives.

Finally, please know that my prayers are with you as you embark on this new stage in your precious daughter's life. This is an exciting time in your life as well as hers. It is my prayer that all the joy, connectedness, and love that God intended to be part of the parent-child relationship be yours.

In Him,
Ami M. Loper

Introduction

Daughter~

Congratulations! You are getting older, changing and growing at a rapid pace. <u>The Miracle of Change</u> is a book for young ladies like you and will pick up where <u>The Miracle of Life</u> left off. Therefore, it will be important that you read or re-read that book first.

My hope, intent, and purpose for this book is that it will be something you and your mother will be reading together. Titus 2:4 tells us that the older women are to teach the younger. You may have several questions based on information you have heard from friends that are not answered in this book. Your mother will probably know the answers and desires to share those with you. Remember, she has been where you are now and she has been where you are going. She is the best person to help guide you through this exciting time in your life. The next few years will be filled with many questions; you will need her wisdom.

Please take your time reading through <u>The Miracle of Change</u>, taking as many breaks as you want. You will receive all the information you desire soon enough. Ask your mother questions throughout the reading and listen to the wisdom she will pass on to you. Please, do not be afraid to speak up if there is something which you do not understand or which is confusing. Since the day you were born, your mother has waited to share this information with you, so she wants to make sure it is clearly understood.

So sit back, sip some hot cocoa or lemonade and prepare yourself for an exciting future of being a woman!

Enjoy!
Ami Loper

Becoming a Woman

"For you created my inmost being; you knit me together in my mother's womb. I praise you because I am fearfully and wonderfully made; your works are wonderful, I know that full well. My frame was not hidden from you when I was made in the secret place. When I was woven together in the depths of the earth, your eyes saw my unformed body. All the days ordained for me were written in your book before one of them came to be."
Psalm 139:13-16.

    Before your mother and father knew you existed, God knew you were there and He had a plan! Long before that, before your parents even existed, He planned that you would be born. He wants you here on Earth for a very special reason. Only God can show you what that special reason is, but we do know one part of God's plan is that you would be a girl!

    Being a girl and becoming a woman are very precious gifts from God. There are so many exciting and joyful aspects of being a girl - as I'm sure you're already discovering. Being a girl means that you are versatile, adaptable, and multi-talented! You can dig in the dirt and then go paint your fingernails. You can put on jeans and an old shirt and work in the yard and then transform yourself into a beauty in a lovely dress. You can play basketball and then dance like a ballerina. Girls are special that way! Most importantly, girls are special to God. He created us for great things that no one and nothing else in all creation could accomplish before He made us.

God says in Proverbs 31:10 that a woman is more valuable than jewels. He says women of God are strong and brave (v. 17, 25) and yet sensitive and kind (v. 20). God says we are trustworthy (v. 11), hard workers (v. 13, 15), wise (v. 16, 18, 26), and creative (v. 19, 22). God says women who trust in Him are worthy of admiration (v. 30, 31).

Yes, being a girl is a precious gift indeed. This is not to say boys are not precious as well! God has a special plan for them, too. However, God wants us, as girls, to be thankful for the way He chose to make us. He wants us to know that He loves women very much.

When Jesus was on Earth, He spent much of His very valuable time showing the world that women are precious to God. Jesus talked to many women, which people thought men of His position should not do. However, in John 4, Jesus talked to the "woman at the well" just to let her know how valuable she was to Him. This gesture shocked His disciples, and the woman too, but it showed us a portion of God's heart toward women.

He also talked to many sick women and healed them (Matthew 8:14-15, Mark 5:24-34, Mark 7:25-30, Luke 13:10-17). He even said certain women would be remembered and honored for all time (Luke 1:28, Matthew 26:6-13).

Just as God loved these women, so He also loves you. He has chosen you to be a woman of God!

Back to the Flower

"Consider how the lilies grow. They do not labor or spin. Yet I tell you, not even Solomon in all his splendor was dressed like one of these. If that is how God clothes the grass of the field, which is here today, and tomorrow is thrown into the fire, how much more will he clothe you...?"
Luke 12:27-28

  God does clothe us day to day; but more than this, He has clothed us in His love and a purpose that far exceeds the purpose of a flower. God took great care in your creation.

  Flowers certainly are incredible creations of God. There is so much they can teach us about ourselves. Now that you are older, we are going to look at the flower more closely and see more of the application it has for us as girls.

  Let's begin by thinking of your mother and your father as that first flower. The long, fuzzy stems in the center of the flower are the father part of the flower. In the flower, this father part is called the stamen and the pollen on the ends of the stamen represent the father's half of the seed.

  Next to the stamen is the carpel, which represents the mother part of the flower. When the pollen is transferred to the carpel, it makes a path into the carpel and down into the flower. The pollen then reaches a portion of the flower called the **ovary** where the egg is stored. The **egg** is the mother's half of the seed. When the pollen and the egg join, they become a new, complete seed that will grow until it is ready to be released. When a new flower seed is 'born,' it falls to the ground or is carried off by the wind to become a new plant.

When the new seed is in the ground, it begins by putting down roots and then, before long, a tiny bit of green pops up above the earth's surface. It is a seedling! This young plant will grow and grow until it is ready to start making flowers of its own. This will be an exciting and beautiful time in the plant's life and is very much like your life! For nine months you grew inside your mother until you were born and began a new life of your own. For all these years, you have been growing in the nurturing shade of your parents until you become mature, wise, and married, ready to start the cycle of a new family all over again.

Changes

"There is a time for everything, and a season for every activity under heaven."
Ecclesiastes 3:1

In the same way that a plant changes from a seedling into a flower-producing plant, your body will also go through some changes. The changes begin when the **pituitary gland**, which is located in your brain, tells your body what changes to make and when. It is like an alarm clock for your body.

Just as God created flowers to grow and blossom at different times and in different seasons, He created each girl to blossom at her own unique time. Some girls will start to change at around nine or ten years old and others will start when they are fifteen or sixteen. There is nothing wrong with starting earlier or later. God has preset the alarm clock that tells your body when it is the right time for *you* to start changing. There is nothing you can do to rush it or slow it down.

One of the first noticeable changes is that your **perspiration** (or sweat) begins to smell bad and you may have some **blemishes** (or pimples) on your face. Now is the time to pay even closer attention to cleanliness. Your mom will assist you in finding products like deodorant and special soaps for girls your age to help you smell and look your best.

Another change that occurs is the growth of hair on different parts of your body. You will begin to have more hair on your legs and it may be darker. You will also begin to have hair growing on your underarms and around your private area. These may seem like strange places to have hair right now, but this hair growth is normal and will be there all your life.

You will begin to notice slow changes taking place with the shape of your body, from head to toe. First, you will begin to notice the development of breasts. This process will happen rather slowly over a period of five to eight years. You may notice that your breasts are a little sore at times and they feel different. The dark part of the breast, called the **areola**, may become a little darker, too. You and your mother will find this a special time to shop for a bra so you will be decent and more comfortable.

You will also notice that your waist begins to trim while your hips begin to become wider, giving you less of a girl's shape and more of a woman's shape. These changes are not very noticeable at first, but over time you will begin to see that your clothes fit a little differently. In addition, your legs will lengthen, making you taller and your feet will grow to support your body. These new developments are all part of the changing and growing it is now time for you to experience. We call this time of changes in a girl's life "**puberty**."

One More Change

"(God) changes times and seasons."
Daniel 2:21

While there are changes you can see taking place on the outside, there will also be changes starting deep inside your body that you are not able to see. Just like that growing plant, you have put down your roots and are growing tall and strong. Soon you will start to produce flowers!

Now, "producing flowers" does not mean that you will soon have babies. No, that is for much later. Like a plant with flowers, most of the time, those flowers do not turn into seeds and baby plants. They simply have flowers that will bloom for a short time and then the flower will fade away.

Nearly all plants cycle this way. Branches bud; they bloom into flowers and then they slowly wilt and blow away. Then the process starts all over again. The branch buds, then blooms, then the blossom withers.

It is as if the plant is practicing for the time when it will one day produce another plant by making a seed. Your body will begin to do a similar thing. Inside your body, in the lower part of your abdomen, is your **womb** (**uterus**). Your womb is the place God created for a baby to someday grow inside you after you are married. But for now, your body starts practicing - just like the young plant that is starting to have flowers.

Let's take a look at the special unseen parts God created in you that will make all this happen. First, you have a pair of **ovaries** where eggs are developed. The eggs are tiny, about the size of a small grain of sand. The two ovaries are located one on each side of your womb. God placed all the eggs you will ever have within the ovaries while you were still inside your mother's womb!

Now that your body is maturing, the eggs are also maturing. When this happens, we say the egg is "ripe" like fruit on a tree, ready to be picked. Each month, one of your ovaries forms a small bubble and the ripe egg is released. This process is called, "**ovulation**."

The little egg's next destination is the **Fallopian tube**. There are two of these also. The Fallopian tube forms a pathway between each ovary and the womb. At the end of the Fallopian tubes, are small hair-like fringes called **fimbria** that guide the egg from the ovary into the tube. The egg is then led through the Fallopian tube by small projections until it reaches the womb.

This whole process has taken about a week. During this time, the womb has been very busy. Let's back up and see what has been happening there.

All this time, your body has been preparing the womb for the arrival of the egg. Your body does this as practice for the time, after you are married, when the egg will not simply be an egg anymore, but will have joined with the daddy half of the seed, becoming a baby. For now, your body is just practicing.

As a Mama bird lines her nest with soft leaves and feathers so her babies will have a nice comfortable place to grow, your body has also been preparing a **lining** for your womb. Just as a bird uses what is available to her to make a lining, so your body uses what it has available. The lining of your womb will be made of bodily tissue and blood. This lining covers the inside of the womb and makes it a soft place for a baby.

When the egg finally arrives from the Fallopian tube, your body will realize it is just an egg and not a baby. At this point, the dying egg releases **hormones**, or chemicals, that will cause the lining of the womb to fall away and be cleaned out. The blood and tissue that made up the lining will slowly flow out of your body at your private area.

This flow is called **menstruation** or "having a **period**." It generally lasts 2 - 8 days. A week or so after your menstrual period is over, the process starts all over again. Another "ripe" egg is released from an ovary and the lining begins to build up all over again - just the way a plant produces flowers over and over again! God created your body this way so that you might be able to one day participate with Him in the miraculous creation of a baby.

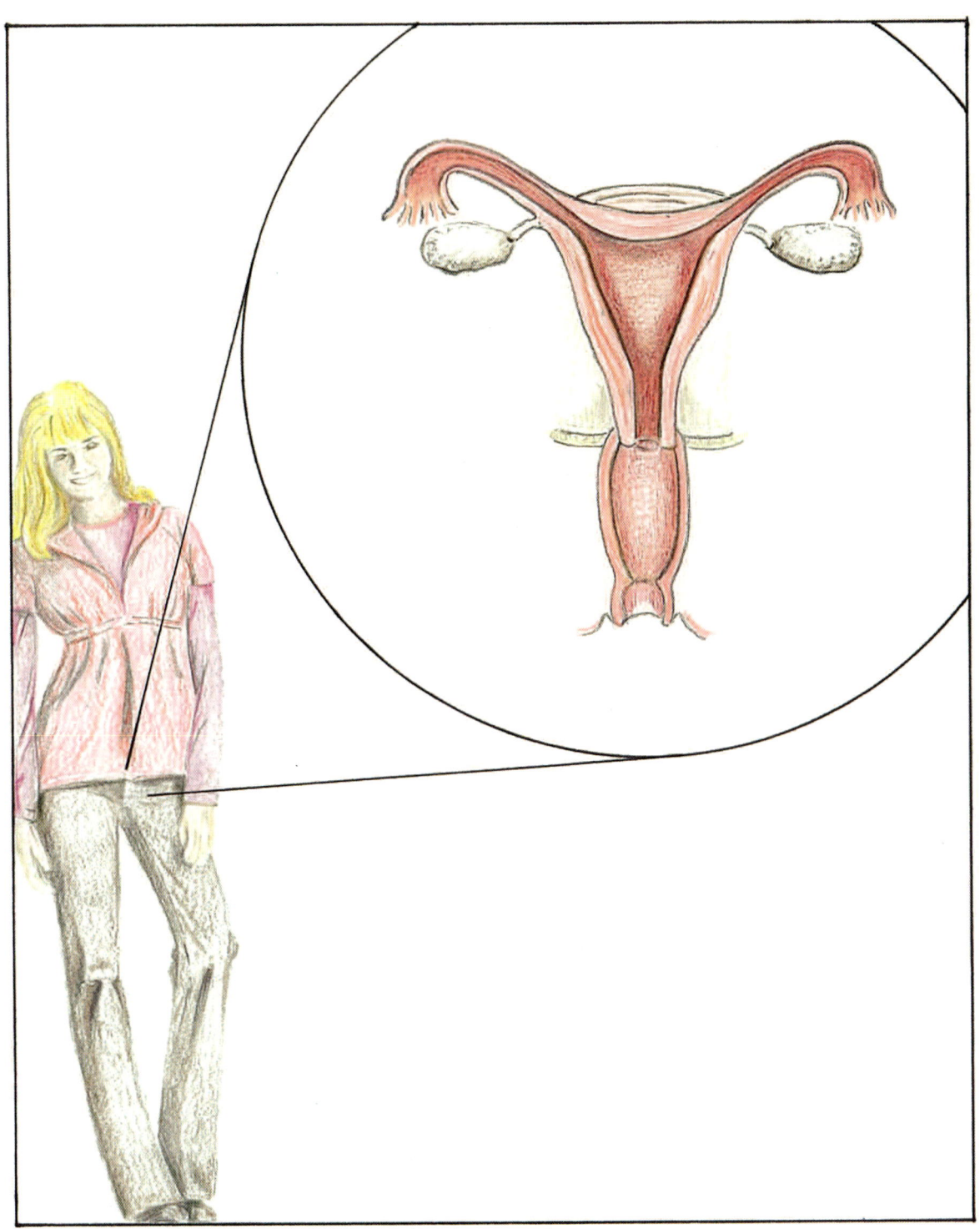

Things to Know

"An honest answer is like a kiss…"
Proverbs 24:26

By now, you are probably bubbling over with questions! Although we will attempt to answer them in this section, please remember, your mom would love to hear your questions and certainly can provide answers as well! Here are some common questions:

"How often will all this happen?"

Only God knows when a girl will have her first period, but once she has had a few periods, a pattern usually develops. When you first start to have your periods, it may take awhile for them to regulate, or come in a predictable pattern. Some girls may even have one or two periods and then nothing for several months. It is a good idea to keep track of your periods on a personal calendar so you can begin to see a pattern or cycle and be less surprised when your period starts.

<u>Cycles</u> are measured by counting the number of days from the start of one period to the start of the next. This time period is one "cycle." Though the length of cycles varies from woman to woman, each woman's cycle becomes fairly predictable. As a general guideline, cycles can range from 26 - 35 days long.

"Does this flow, or 'discharge,' happen all at once?"

No, it doesn't. Usually, the first day will start with a reddish-brown or pinkish flow, which will change to a darker red over the next few days then back to a reddish-brown or pink the last day. You may be thinking that this is a lot of fluid, but in reality, it is only about seven tablespoons.

It is important to know that most girls also have a small amount of <u>discharge</u> between their periods and even before their periods ever start.

This discharge is creamy in color. It is part of God's plan to keep your body clean and comfortable.

"How do I keep myself clean during my period?"

In order to keep yourself and your clothing clean during your period, the use of **feminine protection** will be an important part of personal hygiene. Generally you will wear **pads** or sanitary napkins that will be placed in your underwear to absorb the flow. These pads or napkins will need to be changed frequently to prevent the discharge from leaking out onto your clothes. Pads should be changed at least twice a day so you stay clean and smelling fresh.

Another form of protection to use during your 'period' is called a **tampon**. Tampons are placed inside the body to absorb the menstrual flow. Tampons can be a little difficult to use and dangerous if used improperly. Waiting several months or even years in order to become very knowledgeable about how your body will cycle is usually a good choice. Discussing the use of tampons with your mother is wise so a decision can be made about what is best for you.

Taking extra care regarding your personal hygiene by bathing or showering at least once a day during your period is also very important. Should clothing or bed sheets become soiled, ask your mother for help in cleaning up appropriately. Also discuss with your mother the best way to dispose of your feminine protection. Discretion is very important in this area, particularly if you have younger siblings in your home—and don't forget about Dad!

"What about my emotions?"

Some girls, or their parents, notice that the week before the start of a period, a girl feels especially emotional. Normally, things which make you happy and laugh can suddenly make you cry tears of joy. Things that make you frustrated or sad can seem overwhelming. These reactions are due to all the hormones used by your body to move your cycle along. You may have heard this time called "**Pre-Menstrual Syndrome**" or "**P.M.S.**"

To gain self-control over these emotions it is helpful to understand and recognize why you feel this way. That realization will assist you in putting your emotions into perspective. The next and most valuable thing you should do is pray. Ask the Lord to help you know the truth about your feelings and to comfort you. Talking to your parents about how you are feeling is wise as this will help them be better equipped to understand the way you're feeling and support you in prayer. You will always feel better after you talk out your feelings with those who love you so much. Putting off any major decisions for about a week is a good idea as these hormones being produced in your body can sometimes make you see things in a distorted light. Please remember, this time of adjustment should never be used as an excuse for rude behavior.

"Is having a 'period' painful?"

Though there is blood coming from inside your body, you will be glad to know you are not "bleeding." Having your period does not hurt like having a cut. Some girls experience cramping in their lower abdomen the first day or two of their period. **Cramping** does not mean anything is wrong; it is just the womb **contracting** (tightening) to help release the fluid from your body. If the cramps make you feel uncomfortable, you can try putting your feet up or lying down. Some find the use of a heating pad helpful. Should these comfort measures not be helpful, talk to your Mom as there are medications especially designed to help minimize any possible discomfort from menstrual cramps. And, make sure you tell yourself that you will feel better tomorrow!

"Must I stop all my normal activities when having my period?"

An important fact to remember is that although your periods come and go, life goes on! During your period, maintaining your normal activity level is okay, and even good for you. Some of the best things you can do for yourself during all of your cycle, are to eat right, exercise, and get enough rest. Drink plenty of water and add some iron-rich foods to your diet. First Corinthians 3:16 tells us that our bodies are God's temple and we ought to care for them. Taking care of yourself is always the best way to stay healthy and feel good!

"How long will I have periods?"

Periods will not last your entire life. Eventually, your ovaries will run out of eggs and your periods will slowly stop. This phase is called **menopause** and will happen when you are in your 40's or 50's. Until that time, you will continue to have periods each month, unless you are pregnant. Naturally, when you are pregnant, the lining in your womb will be kept there to provide protection for your baby.

"Does having my period mean I'm ready to have a baby?"

Much more goes into being ready to have a baby than just having your period. Much time must pass before everything falls in line and you are ready to have a child of your own. Many physical changes will take place. Many emotional and mental changes and developments must also take place. You must finish your education. You must grow older and wiser. Once all these changes are in place, God will send you a husband who is also mature in all these ways. Once you are married, the two of you, with God, will decide when the right time for you to have children will be.

Though you will likely have between 400 and 450 periods during your lifetime, you will not be having that many children nor will you be pregnant continuously! Having your period only means that your body is beginning to be ready for when God will bring you children. God has appointed a time for each woman to have the babies she will have.

Being a Beautiful Girl

"Catch for us the foxes, the little foxes that ruin the vineyards, our vineyards that are in bloom."
Song of Solomon 2:15

*"The thief comes only to steal and kill and destroy;
I have come that they may have life,
and have it to the full."*
John 10:10

Every single girl is beautiful. God has created each one to have a special something all her own. All girls have their own unique spark that lights up their world. Knowing deeply in her heart that she is precious and beautifully created by her loving and perfect Creator serves to make a girl's beauty shine more radiantly.

Every flower is also beautiful. Each is unique and so varied, with different colors, shapes, and smells. God created each one beautiful in its own special way. Flowers don't need to be the same to be beautiful; in fact, much of their beauty lies in their variety and uniqueness.

Similarly, people are not supposed to look or act alike. It would be a bland and boring world if they did! Your individuality is a gift from God. In spite of this, you may feel awkward or out of place if what makes you unique seems different than what makes the girl next to you unique. It is very common to feel that you must look or act or dress like others. This feeling can become a trap that steals your uniqueness. Don't give away that which makes you special! Hold on to it! Don't be willing to become a clone or an exact copy of others! Be confident that God made you a one-of-a-kind on purpose — and you are a beautiful girl - inside and out.

Even beautiful growing things have enemies and, sad to say, you are no different. Some animals must be kept out of a garden or they will quickly make the fruits of your labor their meal! Just as a gardener puts a pretty fence around his garden to protect his growing plants, so the Great Gardener of us all, God, has placed a protective hedge around you. This hedge consists of your parents, God's rules for right living, and the wisdom God gives you on how to carry out those rules.

God knows that "your enemy the devil prowls around like a roaring lion looking for someone to devour." (1 Peter 5:8) This lion knows he cannot get to you as long as you are safe and secure behind the Gardener's fence, so he will try to lure you from your protected haven. His lures can be powerful forces for all ages, but when you are growing up and trying to decide who you are, they can be even more powerful.

The enemy doesn't like the beauty of women because he knows that we are intended to reflect the beauty of God. The enemy may try to tempt and convince you to come away from the Gardener's view of what true beauty is by using the lures of popularity and acceptance from your peers. Often he attempts to twist what beauty truly is so that our appearance no longer reflects and glorifies God's beauty, but the enemy's false idea of beauty.

God's beauty is brilliantly stunning with a serene confidence, but the enemy's twisted beauty is obnoxious and arrogant. God's beauty in women reveals His beauty and His sweet nature, while the enemy's twisted beauty changes the focus to the person or that person's physical attributes. God's beauty is pure and loving, but the enemy's twisted beauty is selfish and harms the person trying to attain it and those who are attracted by it.

Keeping the real beauty, God's beauty, in your physical appearance is a matter of the heart. Looking your best is an admirable goal. Reflecting God's beauty by trying to hide your own would be impossible! But listen to your heart. Is the motivation for what you wear or the way you act to attract attention to your body or do you just want to look nice? Be honest with yourself.

In Proverbs, God explains to us that though a woman may be very beautiful, she can actually choose to dress and behave in a way that makes her look ridiculous and her beauty is wasted. He says, "Like a gold ring in a pig's snout is a beautiful woman who shows no discretion." (Proverbs 11:22) Discretion means to be wise, being careful to not be foolish. Just as the beauty of a gold ring is wasted when given to a pig, so beauty is wasted when a girl lacks the wisdom to protect and treasure it. God is warning us that though we may be very beautiful, we can abuse our beauty by allowing ourselves to become attached to unclean, unwise behaviors.

The good news is that the opposite is also true. When we abide (or stay close to) Jesus, we can keep our hearts pure. And with our hearts pure, Jesus will give us the wisdom and discretion to keep our minds and bodies pure as well. We won't have to worry about whether or not what we're wearing fits "the rules." Our desire to keep a pure heart will make us want to dress appropriately.

Sometimes when you look in the mirror, you may wonder if you are beautiful. The truth is, you are. Of course, beauty comes from so much more than the structure of your face or your shape or knowing how to do your hair in the latest style. People used to say beauty is only skin deep, but they were wrong! Beauty, true beauty, is much deeper than skin. Beauty comes from deep inside. When a girl has purity in her heart and she knows without a doubt that Jesus, her Savior, loves her beyond her wildest dreams, beauty will naturally flow out of her. It has been said that there is nothing as beautiful as confidence and when that confidence is rooted in knowing who you are as God's glorious creation, this saying is true. A girl who glows with the joy and reassurance of God's love is the most beautiful girl in the world! What is felt in her heart shows up on her face.

The Abiding Flower

"I am the vine; you are the branches. If a man remains in me and I in him, he will bear much fruit; apart from me you can do nothing."
John 15:5

Though it's true that flowers are beautiful, there is a way to diminish the beauty of a flower, a way to steal its splendor. If you cut a flower from the stem it is growing on, depriving it of the water and nutrients it desperately needs, the flower will soon wilt. As you grow and change into a young woman, it is important to stay connected to your root system: Jesus. Now is the time to develop your own relationship with God, independent of your parents' relationship with Him. Allowing God to nurture you with His Word and through times of prayer and worship will help you to fully develop into the woman He designed you to be. Take the time and effort to keep this most important relationship alive.

The second most important relationship you'll have as you develop into a woman is with your parents. They are like the larger, more mature plant that offers its protection to the seedling. You are that seedling. Their desire is that, as much as it is possible, you experience all the good things of life while they give you shelter from the sweltering noonday sun and the battering winds. A young plant that tries to grow too far from a sheltering plant will wither or grow slowly.

When Eve was being tempted in the garden, one of the first ways the serpent tempted her was to twist God's words and make Eve think that God wasn't giving her all she deserved. He began by causing Eve to look at the things she could not do. He said, "Did God really say, 'You must not eat from any tree in the garden'?"

Of course, God had given them all the trees except one, but the serpent caused Eve to focus only on that one tree. Eve began to be like a beautiful plant in the garden which forgot the beauty around her and began to focus on the fence - thinking the fence was keeping her from good things instead of realizing that the only thing the fence was keeping her from was destruction.

All people experience the temptation to look at what they can't have instead of all they do have and I'm sure you are no different. Have you ever heard the enemy tempting you? Perhaps, like Eve, you've been tempted to think that you can run your own life better than those in authority over you. Maybe you've had thoughts that God or your parents just don't want you to have any fun. Maybe you've been tempted to compromise your standards to fit in with kids at school or even at church. These thoughts are all ways the enemy tries to lure you out of the protection of your fenced garden home.

But abiding in God's love and protection will keep you far from harm and growing strong and free to be all the wonderful things God wants you to be. Trusting the parents God selected for you to want what is best for you will give you a sense of calm reassurance. You are surrounded by those who love you the most in the world! Stay in the garden.

Conclusion

"I urge you to live a life worthy of the calling you have received."
Ephesians 4:1

    As you go through life, you will hear many other people's points of view about being a woman and all that goes with it. In all that you hear, make sure you are listening to the Only Voice that really matters: God's! When people do not listen to who God says they are, they can get very confused and begin to misunderstand their own purpose.
    Though others may say femininity isn't valuable, God says its value outweighs jewels (Proverbs 31:10). Though some may say being a pure woman is meaningless, God says the pure are pleasing to Him (Proverbs 15:26). Though some may say only the outward appearance is important, we know God looks on our hearts (1 Samuel 16:7). Though some call menstruation a curse, we can trust that our womanhood is a gift from God (Genesis 1:27).
    Congratulations! God has chosen you to be a woman!

Aloe

Saguaro Cactus

Milkweed

Sunflower

Clematis

Rose

Lily

Forsythia

Glossary

Though the following words may have other meanings than those listed below, these are the meanings as they pertain to this book.

<u>areola</u> - the dark area on the breast surrounding the nipple.
<u>blemishes</u> - pimples or sores on the face.
<u>contract</u> - the tightening of the womb.
<u>cramp</u> - a feeling of tightness and pain in the lower abdomen.
<u>cycle</u> - the number of days from the first day of one period to the first day of the next period.
<u>discharge</u> - the fluid that flows out of your body either during the period or between periods.
<u>egg</u> - the mother part of the seed that is developed in the ovary. It will either join with the father part of the seed to become a baby or will flow out of the body along with the menstrual flow.
<u>Fallopian tubes</u> - the pathways from each ovary to the womb.
<u>feminine protection</u> - the supplies a girl wears during her period to protect her clothing.
<u>fimbria</u> - the fringe-like opening at the end of each Fallopian tube.
<u>hormones</u> - chemicals produced in the body that cause changes to occur in the body.
<u>lining</u> - the build up of blood and bodily tissue on the inside walls of the womb.
<u>menopause</u> - the time in a woman's life when her periods cease, occurring, on average, at age 51.
<u>menstruation</u> - the flow of blood and tissue from the uterus.
<u>ovary</u> - a small gland on either side of the womb where eggs are developed and stored until ovulation.
<u>ovulation</u> - the time when the developed egg comes out of the ovary.
<u>pads</u> - a form of feminine protection which has a sticky backing that is pressed into the underwear.

period - the flow of blood and tissue from the uterus.
perspiration - sweat
pituitary gland - a small gland in the brain that sends out hormones that cause growth and change.
pre-menstrual syndrome (PMS) - approximately the week preceding the menstrual cycle when hormones are particularly high sometimes causing mood swings and irritability.
puberty - the time of physical changes in a young person's life.
tampons - a form of feminine protection that is placed inside the body to absorb the menstrual flow. If used irresponsibly, tampons may cause Toxic Shock Syndrome, sometimes leading to death.
uterus - the fist-sized organ in a girl's body where babies may grow after marriage.
womb - another name for uterus.